THE IONA COMMUNITY STORY

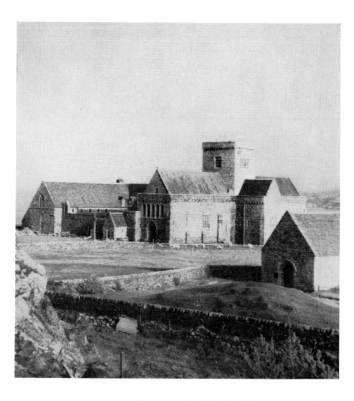

IONA, the restored Abbey buildings

THE IONA
COMMUNITY STORY

by

T. RALPH MORTON

LUTTERWORTH PRESS
LONDON

Printed in Great Britain by
Wyman & Sons, Ltd., London, Fakenham and Reading

CONTENTS

Chapter One

INTRODUCING IONA

MEN have been coming to Iona for centuries. Since St. Columba landed on Iona in A.D. 563 it has been a place of pilgrimage. And perhaps it was so even before that, in its pagan days. Perhaps that was why Columba came. Certainly in the years that followed his coming Iona was a place from which men went and to which men came. From Iona men went out as missionaries to the near-by islands and then to the northern mainland and, later, farther afield, to the North of England and to Northern Europe. To Iona kings came for counsel and warriors to find rest and young men for education. And to this day all that remains in visible token of that period of Iona's greatest activity and fame are the crosses of the saints whom they most honoured—St. John and St. Martin—and the graves of the kings, and the well from which they drew water.

The island of Iona lies off the west coast of Scotland, to the west of the Ross of Mull. It is separated from Mull by the Sound of Iona, a stretch of water about a mile broad. Beyond is the open Atlantic. The island is about three miles long from north to south and about a mile and a half broad at its broadest point.

7

The story of The Iona Community has much to do with the island of Iona. It is indeed centred on Iona, but the story of The Iona Community has to do not only with Iona. It is not the story of Iona. That is a longer and an older story.

When in the eleventh century the Roman Church took over from the Celtic, the Iona we know to-day began to take shape. It was in this period that the buildings which we now see were built. And still Iona remained a place of pilgrimage, holy because of its ancient past and holy through the devotions of the men and women who lived there.

The end came to that period with the Reformation. The religious community was dispersed. The buildings decayed into ruins. But still Iona remained a place of which the name was treasured and to which men were drawn. Even when travel was hard and the island could offer nothing better in the way of accommodation than straw in a shed, stray travellers still came to Iona. In the eighteenth century Dr. Johnson came, not without difficulty, determined to visit one of the places that the devotion of men had made most sacred. With him came Boswell, who was moved to prayer. And they were by no means the only ones who braved the journey.

When with the Victorian age ease and speed of transport made travel possible for the many, the crowds began to come to Iona. They were now called tourists and the enticement of the trip was rather the geology of

Staffa than the antiquity of Iona. But even to them Iona was a place of pilgrimage which spoke of a strange past.

The story of Iona is the history of Scotland. All the centuries of known Scottish history are reflected in its story.

To-day men still come to Iona. Indeed, they come in greater numbers than ever before. Many come as tourists, but gain a new consciousness of being on a pilgrimage. It is no longer the geology of Staffa that draws them but Iona itself—the past of Iona and what is happening on Iona to-day.

And more significant than those who come in their thousands to look at Iona are those who now come once again to Iona to build and those who once again go out from Iona to work in Christ's name elsewhere. Once again there are masons and joiners erecting buildings on Iona to the Glory of God and for the use of His Church. Once again men and women inspired by Iona are to be found in Africa and Asia as missionaries of Christ's Church. Once again men—ministers and laymen—re-gather on Iona to discuss their missionary work at home and abroad. Once again men from other lands and from other Churches come to share in the life and in the work on Iona. And—novel to Iona and symbol of the new age in which we live—hundreds of young people, mainly from the cities, come each year to camp on Iona and to find the centre of their life in the worship of the Abbey.

This is the newest stage in the long and varied history of Iona. This is the story of The Iona Community. It links up with all that has gone before in the history of Iona and yet it is new and distinct. This is seen in the work of building in which The Iona Community is engaged. It is the latest stage in that work of building and rebuilding that has been going on upon Iona for centuries. The work is on the old foundations and, perhaps as in no earlier period of the building, seeks to take up and incorporate what has gone before. And yet the work is carried out in conscious preparation for a quite new world and expects for the building a different use from anything it has known in the past.

The Iona Community story is certainly centred on Iona but it is not only about Iona. This is, indeed, true of all the greater phases of Iona's story. The story of Iona has always been about those who have come from elsewhere and of those who have gone to other parts. For Iona is still the island of Columba who came from Ireland and of his men whose desire it was that foreign soil should be over them at the end.

Chapter Two

THE BEGINNING OF THE STORY

THE story of The Iona Community begins in 1938 in Govan.

The year and the place are significant.

The year is 1938. To us to-day that is the year before the War. To people at that time it was another year of unemployment for millions of men in this country. They did not know that it was to be the last year of unemployment; that a war was coming to end unemployment. They knew it only as yet another in a long series of years of depression.

The place is Govan. The history of the Church in Govan goes back to Columba's time. For centuries it was a country village and a mighty parish until with industrial expansion Glasgow grew and swallowed it up in its greater mass. Govan to-day depends on shipbuilding. And in the 'thirties shipbuilding, with the other heavy industries, was most cruelly hit by the depression. Govan suffered as few other places did. Eighty per cent of the men of Govan were unemployed and had been so for years. It is difficult for us, whose troubles have been of a different sort, to appreciate what it means to know that you are highly skilled and that on your skill the wealth of your country has been built and to realize that you are now unwanted, that there is no work for you and not enough food and no future for your children. In those circumstances men become suspicious of those in authority and cynical about the Church, for easy words are no help.

You must go to Iona if you would see The Iona Community. Indeed, you must go to Iona and live there for a time if you would become a member of The Iona Community. If you want at all to understand The Iona Community you are well advised to visit Iona. But you will never understand The Iona Community fully unless you realize something of what "Govan, 1938" means. If that is something quite incomprehensible, then The Iona Community will remain a mystery. And the trouble is that, while you can visit Iona any year, you cannot revisit "Govan, 1938" except in the imagination.

This is, of course, only to say that The Iona Community is like a person. It is rooted in space and time. It has its origin in a particular place in a particular year. It is not based on a theory or tied to a principle, however tempting it may be to its members to produce principles and theories as counters in the theological game. Its inquirers and its critics would find it much more intelligible if The Iona Community could point to a principle instead of to a date. Then they could discuss the correctness of the principle and whether The Iona Community lived up to it. Then, indeed, there would be an easy answer to the innumerable questions that men ask: "Why don't you do this? Why don't you do that? Why are there no doctors in The Iona Community? Why don't you have women members? Surely the ideal community should include every type of person?" The only answer is that The Iona Community came into existence in Govan in 1938. If it were independent of place and time, if it were based upon the perfect theory, then indeed it might be the perfect society. But it would not have begun with the members with which it started. It would not have begun in Govan in 1938.

It came into existence because of what was happening in Govan in 1938. And what was happening then determined its form, its membership, its activities and its history. The explanation of many of the things that puzzle people about The Iona Community is to be found there. And perhaps The Iona Community will always remain a bit of a mystery for many people just because its origin in Govan is so much forgotten and cannot be recovered.

But it is not, of course, the date and the place alone that can explain The Iona Community. The date and the place were shared by thousands. There were many people at that time concerned about the unemployed. There were many in the Church concerned about the witness of the Church. Time and place were not unique. Time and place were not enough. There was need of a person to whom the time and the place were an inescapable challenge. That person was George MacLeod, the only originator of The Iona Community.

"Govan 1938" challenged his compassion, his vision and his courage. It was his uncomfortable possession of these three qualities that led him to found The Iona Community. The compassion that the needs of men in Govan aroused was no detached philanthropy, no disinterested affection. When once he was heard telling a group of Borstal boys: "We are no better than you: it's just that we haven't been found out", those who heard him felt that he was speaking in an exaggerated and highly dangerous way and that, in any case, he didn't really mean it. But he did mean it. He meant that the rest of us have not been tested as these boys had been tested and therefore we have not been found out. His compassion arises from understanding. His compassion challenged him to see what could be done. His vision was not, as with so many of us, a dream of what could be done if the impossible happened: of what could be done if only . . . His vision was always expressed in what could and must be done immediately. It was linked to a detailed plan of action, to the embarrassment of many. His courage is the courage of the man who is not afraid of what others think and who can make great demands upon himself.

George MacLeod had come to be minister of the Old Parish of Govan in 1930, at the beginning of the worst period of the depression. He came from Edinburgh, from the Parish of St. Cuthbert's, one of Edinburgh's largest and most famous churches. People wondered why he moved from St. Cuthbert's and from all to which it might have led. But fundamentally he was coming home. He was coming home to the West to which he belonged by his inheritance. He was coming home to the city in which he had been brought up and to which his immediate family belonged, for his father had been one of Glasgow's members of Parliament and his grandfather, Norman MacLeod, its most outstanding minister of last century. He was coming home too to the men with whom he had found community in the Argyll and Sutherland Highlanders during the First World War. And deliberately he came to Govan because he knew that in this kind of place was the real challenge to the Church to-day.

His eight years in Govan had been years of experiment and achievement. His greatest achievements were probably in the sphere of public worship: in the beauty, power and relevance which he brought to the revitalizing of worship; in the way in which through broadcasting he brought to many a new hope; in his ability to make men find in prayer a real activity. His experiments were in the service of the unemployed. He opened clubs for them. He provided work for them: they relaid the graveyard and the grounds round the church as a seemly open space. And one of the most prophetic things that he did was to take over an old disused mill in the hills to the south of Glasgow and by the labour of unemployed men to turn it into a youth hostel for the use of their sons at the week-ends.

In the eyes of the Church and of the world his ministry at Govan was a conspicuously successful one. And it was; but not in the ways that people thought. It was a creative ministry because of the discovery of new lines of approach and because of the realization that much that was conventional and outwardly successful was already dead.

It was, therefore, a surprise to most people in the Church when he resigned his parish and gave up this most successful ministry. They saw the Church in Govan to be successful, well attended and active. They could not see what more its minister wanted to do or to get. What was happening to men was far more important than what was happening to the Church. What was happening to men was what mattered to Christ and should matter to His Church. And in terms of the particular responsibility of the Church in Govan, failure to meet the needs of the men of the parish could not be offset by success in attracting those outside. The Church was failing because it was so successful and so respectable. It was not that men did not appreciate the social work done for them. It was useful work and it had to be done for its own sake but it did not lead men into the Church. And it was not that men did not understand what the Church was saying; far less reject it. They had no quarrel with what the Church was saying. They only doubted whether the Church meant or even understood what she was saying. Perhaps they saw the Gospel in too simple a light. Certainly they did not see the Gospel reflected in the life of the Church. Above all they did not feel that they mattered to the Church.

The restoration of Fingalton Mill, the old mill in the hills to the south of Glasgow, was somehow different. It was not something that was done for them. It was something that had been done with them. It was, indeed, something that they had done for others. Fingalton Mill meant more for the future than all the crowded services.

George MacLeod resigned his charge because he believed that some radical reformation of the Church's life and work was needed. Merely to revivify the old conventional pattern would not be enough. It would not be enough to add new techniques to make it more efficient. It would not be enough to evolve a simpler language and to find new words in which to express the Faith. New techniques would, indeed, have to be found and the need for a new language intelligible to men to-day was urgent. But without some radical reform in the life of the Church all these attempts would be useless. And if there was to be reform there must first be experiment.

George MacLeod resigned his charge because he believed that for all her apparent success the Church was failing in her task. If that had been all, he would have resigned and that would have been the end. He resigned his charge because he believed in the Church and in the future. He resigned because be believed that there were things that the Church could be doing now and which the Church must be doing now. He resigned in order to found The Iona Community. He started The Iona Community because he believed that there must be some body in the Church that was willing to experiment and to make mistakes for the sake of the Church. He started The Iona Community because he believed that it was his duty to make the experiment and not to talk about the need of people making experiments.

It was thus out of the situation in Govan in 1938 and out of George MacLeod's response to that situation that The Iona Community came into existence. Without the place, the time and the man, it cannot be understood. To us looking back it may seem that the situation as then seen in Govan was too simple. It may seem to many that the remedy—this small community—was trivial and not much more than a toy. This might have been so but for two things. One was that the situation out of which The Iona Community was born was a real situation, occupied by real people. It was with the people that George MacLeod was concerned rather than with the situation. These men of Govan and their wives and their children always seem to be there, challenging The Iona Community, judging The Iona Community, supporting The Iona Community. And so long as that is so we cannot escape into the comfortable discussion of theories and the pleasant enjoyment of our own experiences. We are reminded, as were the people of Ezekiel's day, that the sheep of the Lord's pasture are men. And when we begin with that realization we can be led into fuller understanding.

The second thing was that behind the recognition of the practical failure of the Church was the sense of a much deeper failure which yet had in it the promise of far better things. Somehow the Church was missing the true greatness of her Faith.

In every age men have known the exasperation of feeling that they knew in their hearts what the Faith really meant and yet of not being able at all adequately to express it in their lives or to make it intelligible to others in words. That is something that the saints and the prophets have known. It was not this common kind of frustration that was paralysing the Church. It was something much more serious. We had somehow minimized the Faith. We had made it all too intelligible. We had let a screen come down to cut off from us the glory and the wonder and the questioning. We had left ourselves with something the meaning of which we knew exactly and everyone else knew exactly and no one wanted at all. And yet all the time we knew that somewhere, out of sight but not out of reach, was something utterly different—life, glory, power. This was the Faith. But we could not reach it because we would not let it into our ordinary lives where alone it belongs. So the Christian Faith, for all its familiarity, had ceased to be positive and demanding. The Iona

Community began with the conviction that the greater dimensions of the Christian Faith had to be recovered.

Certainly what George MacLeod did for men at that time was a twofold and seemingly incompatible task. He made them see the ordinary life which they accepted as charged with a new meaning, because he helped them to see themselves and to see others really as persons. And at the same time he made them feel that what really mattered was still beyond the horizon.

And so The Iona Community came into being. From the beginning it was faced with a practical task and an impossible quest. But that has been true of the Church at all times.

That combination of a practical task and an impossible quest was evident in the very action in which The Iona Community came to life. George MacLeod resigned his charge and set off for Iona with a dozen young men. Half of them were craftsmen. The other half were young ministers of the Church of Scotland who had just finished their theological training. They set off to re-build the ruined Abbey of Iona and to discover for themselves the way of Christian life for men to-day. They seemed a very casual group. They had not been specially selected for this double task. None was perhaps very sure on what kind of an expedition he was embarking. Most other people thought it was quite mad.

But there was nothing unconsidered or unthought-out in George MacLeod's plans, however much men might call his courage rashness. His plans were well prepared, on paper and in fact. Those responsible for the Abbey had given permission for the rebuilding. Sponsors for his purpose had been found, and willingly found, among the leaders of the Church of Scotland. Among them were Principal David Cairns, Sir D. Y. Cameron, R.A., Sir Iain Colquhoun of Luss, Professor Donald Baillie, Sir David Russell, Dr. John White, to mention only some who are no longer with us. Also nothing material needed for the work that summer on Iona had been forgotten.

And behind the formation of that first small community was the same careful planning. The form it took was based on three convictions.

The first of these convictions was that the way to new life in the Church would be found only by people living and working together. These words—"living and working together"—must be taken at their simplest and fullest meaning. "Living together" does not mean sharing a carefully chosen and defined portion of one's life, as is so often what we mean when we talk of sharing our lives in the Church, where the parts we do not intend to share are as clearly defined, and are the more important. "Living together" must mean sharing the whole of life. And "working together" does not mean co-operating for a short time on some marginal task which makes no great demands. It means working together on the job for which one is paid. It must be ordinary life and daily work, as the world knows both.

The second conviction was that only by so living and working together would men come to understand the fuller nature of the Faith. It was no use beginning with discussion. It was no use imagining that you could think the thing out and then begin to act. Our ways of thinking and of discussion are too individualistic to allow of any progress being made that way. Only through action would understanding come. Action always brings us into touch with other men and we cannot act without learning.

The third conviction arose out of the immediate situation in Govan. That situation revealed the problem of the Church's mission in an industrial society. For the Church, that problem was focused on two groups of men: on the industrial workers and on the ministers. These two groups constituted the two problems for the Church. The industrial worker was a problem because he was not evident in Church and could not be made interested. And if the industrial worker, who is the one in our present society most affected by industrialization, finds no point of contact with the Church, what chance has the Church to make her message heard in the fully industrialized society of the future? And the minister is a problem because he is so much and so exclusively in evidence in the Church that in the eyes of men he is the Church. He at the moment holds the keys that can open the door to life in the Church or keep them shut. A community that is to try to find the way to life for the Church in our new industrial age must include these two groups. It should, indeed, start with these two groups. And such a community is more likely to achieve something if they are not distracted by the presence of others but are left alone to work out their life by themselves, at least at the beginning.

Chapter Three

THE COMING TO IONA

T<small>HE</small> Iona Community began when, after a service of
dedication in Govan Church, George MacLeod, those
who were joining the Community, and the young
architect who was responsible for the huts embarked on
the old coasting steamer *The Dunara Castle* and sailed
down the Clyde. By night they sailed round the Mull
of Kintyre and in a morning of clear sunshine sailed past
Islay and Jura to Iona. There they unloaded the sections
of the huts which they had brought up with them on the
ship. That first summer they lived, ate and slept in one
hut which had already been erected, while they spent
their time laying the foundations and then erecting the
huts which were to be the home of the Community for
the next eighteen years, until in 1956 the east range of the
monastic buildings was finished and they moved in there
to live.

Why did The Iona Community start in such a way?
Why did George MacLeod undertake the completion
of the rebuilding of the ruined Abbey on Iona and make
that the practical work in which The Iona Community
would be engaged? What conceivable connexion
had Govan in 1938, in its depression and unemployment,
with Iona? Why did he go to Iona at all?

Many could not see an answer. They thought the whole thing was mad. Others thought they knew the answer. They knew Iona in the summer as a place of beauty and of peace. Who would go to Iona except for a holiday? This venture, they implied, was really an escape from the demands of the mainland. Or the answer was more sinister. The Iona Community was rebuilding a monastery. What reason could men have to do that unless they meant to become monks and overturn the Reformation in Scotland? So all kinds of rumours spread about the purpose of the new community. And all arose out of the journey to Iona.

Misunderstandings of any new venture are inevitable. It was not to be expected that men should immediately understand and approve George MacLeod's resignation from Govan and his founding of a new Community on Iona to rebuild the ruins there. The proposal to rebuild the ruins of Iona and to make it once again a centre of life and worship did indeed make its appeal to the imaginations of many. But what appealed to their imaginations had often little enough to do with the reasons that brought the Community to Iona and with the needs of the men of Govan. But there never was any doubt in George MacLeod's mind that the Community which found the reason for its existence in Govan must find the centre of its life on Iona. In the second *Coracle*[1] (May, 1939) he wrote: "Surely there

[1] The Journal of the Iona Community, sent out twice yearly to the Friends of the Iona Community.

will always be a spiritual link beyond all reckoning between Govan and Iona."

Why was this? Why did the Community go to Iona?

There were three reasons: an historical reason, a practical one, and a third and lesser one but just as practical.

The first reason that made Iona the inevitable centre of the Community's life was simply the place of Iona in our history. Iona was by no means the first centre of Christian life in Scotland. St. Ninian had built his church "Candida Casa" at Whithorn a hundred and fifty years before St. Columba landed on Iona. But Iona had soon become predominant and had continued as a place of active Christian life for many centuries. It seemed a sad scandal that in the present day the visible tokens of its Christian witness should be in the form of ruins. And it is the length as well as the antiquity of its history that makes Iona impressive. For on Iona the three main strands of that history—the Celtic, the Roman and the Reformed—are evident even to-day. They cannot be forgotten and are waiting to be interwoven in a new unity.

The Celtic period is preserved in the place-names of the island, in ancient stones and tombs and still in the traditions of the people. Columba and his followers seem nearer to us to-day on Iona than the monks of the Middle Ages; perhaps because they made the island so much their own and viewed its beauty more with our eyes.

The Celtic Church is of vital importance to us because it brought the Christian Faith to Scotland. But the way it did this and the kind of Church it established are of as great importance. The Celtic Church did not look on the created universe as evil but as the garment of God's glory. Beauty had its place in worship and in the service of the Church, as the hymns of Columba and the illuminated manuscripts which the Church produced testify. And because it saw the material world as the sphere of God's action the Celtic Church evinced an active concern in all life—in agriculture, in fishing, in education, in politics.

In the life of the Church its emphasis was on corporate life and on individual devotion. It knew nothing of the later separation between the religious and the secular. All life was God's and all members of the Church His servants. The missionary teams that carried the Gospel from Iona to other parts were on the Apostolic model. They were made up of twelve men of various crafts, of whom only two would be priests.

This was the pattern of missionary faith to which Scotland was first converted. Such a total Faith concerned with the totality of life has to be recovered if the Church in Scotland is once again to recover its missionary task. That is the lesson that the first period of Iona's Christian history teaches us. And it is an essential lesson. We have forgotten it. Unless we learn it again we remain unprofitable servants.

The second period, if more foreign to Iona to-day, is

more evident in its visible memorials. The Roman Church which in the eleventh century took over control was less concerned than the Celtic Church in going out from Iona and more concerned in building up a place of retreat to which men and women might come. And so it built larger buildings in more lasting materials. These are the ruins that are being restored to-day. The first to be built and the oldest extant church on the island is the little Norman church in the graveyard. It is associated with the name of St. Margaret, Queen and Reformer, the daughter of Edward the Confessor, King of England, and wife of Malcolm Canmore, King of the Scots. Next to be built was the Nunnery, founded by Reginald, Lord of the Isles. This still stands a ruin. Later was built the Benedictine Monastery which is the building now being restored. These buildings stand as the remaining tokens of the maintenance of a stable life when round these shores swept uncertainty and war and when men must often have sought the shelter of Iona. They are the symbols too of the time when there was but one Church in Christendom and men were not divided in the observance of their faith. That unity in its medieval form is no more recoverable by us than is the form of the Celtic Church. But the unity it knew is as clear a call to us in the Church to-day as is the conception of mission of the Celtic Church. Indeed, the total mission of which the Celtic Church spoke and which is our need to-day can never be achieved until we find a new unity inside the universal Church. This is the second lesson that Iona will not allow us to forget.

The third period of Iona's history began with the Reformation. It began with the closing of the Monastery and of the Nunnery. It witnessed the falling of the buildings into decay and ruin. It was not a period marked by building. Indeed it was not till 1809 that a church was built for the people, the present Parish Church. The Reformers did not regard the ecclesiastical building as the centre of religious life. That centre was to be found in the home. It was not in disregard of the Faith that men paid more attention to their own houses than to church buildings and indeed built their churches in the form of houses. Rather they acted on the Reformation conviction that the centre of ordinary Christian life was in family prayers, that every man's job was his vocation and that political life was under the lordship of Christ. It is an heroic faith, liable to many temptations.

The Celtic and the Roman periods seem strange to us, fascinatingly strange. The Reformation period is now almost as strange to us, but uncomfortably strange. It is the period of which we are the immediate heirs. It is the period to which we belong as we belong to no other, for it has produced us. We are glad and proud to belong to the Reformed Church. But something has gone wrong with our witness. "Govan, 1938" was evidence of that. The centre of the Church's life is no longer in the homes of the people. Worship has become detached from life. The strength of that once heroic faith has been drained. And when the fire of personal conviction, the sense of social solidarity and the recognition of political duty grow dim, then our witness becomes formal, moralistic, dull and irrelevant.

But this period has its demand on us, all the more insistent because we are its immediate heirs. It has its strong part in the witness of Iona; in its call to recover the conviction of personal vocation, not now in isolation but combined with the sense of mission of the Celtic period and the sense of unity of the Roman.

The history of Iona and the hope of Columba's dying prayer:

> Unto this place, small and mean though it be, great homage shall yet be paid not only by the kings and peoples of the Scots, but by the rulers of foreign and barbarous nations and their subjects. In great veneration too shall it be held by holy men of other churches,

offer the first reason why the Iona Community went to Iona and took its name.

The second reason for the choice of Iona was that on Iona there was a task waiting to be finished. It was a task that was significant, symbolic and practicable.

The ruins of the Abbey and of the Nunnery had stood vacant and crumbling since the Reformation. At the very end of last century the Eighth Duke of Argyll handed over the Abbey, the Nunnery and the Reilig Odhrain (the graveyard of the kings) to the Church of

Scotland. In doing so he expressed the hope that the Abbey buildings might be restored and stated explicitly in the Trust Deed that any Christian Church should be free to conduct services according to its own rites in the Abbey.

In the opening years of the century the Abbey Church was restored by public subscription. The last part of the restoration of the church was completed in 1912. From then on the Abbey Church was used for Sunday services in the summer but for the rest of the year stood empty and unused, surrounded by the ruins of the living quarters of the monastery.

The task which George MacLeod undertook as the work of The Iona Community was the completion of the restoration of the whole Abbey. Others had dreamed of the possibility, and tentative suggestions and plans had been made. But George MacLeod's faith and courage were seen, not only in his resignation from his parish and in his gathering together a few men to be a community, but even more in his undertaking personal responsibility for the rebuilding of the Abbey before there was a community and when there were no funds. In that act of faith, and in the willingness to accept what an unknown future would bring, the Iona Community was born.

It was a significant job. It meant the completion of a task on which the Church of Scotland had started. It looked to the day when the Abbey on Iona would not be merely a place where occasional services were held in summer but would be the centre of a full Christian life to which men could come for training and for rest. It was also an immediately significant task in that it was of equal interest to craftsmen and ministers.

The job itself was symbolic of our condition in Scotland to-day. The place of worship had been repaired. The place of men's daily life was in ruins. The Abbey Church had been restored at great expense through the love and devotion of many. It was typical of the present good condition of the church buildings in Scotland, which are probably better cared for and more fully used in worship than ever in the past. But the Church is not only the place of worship. The Church is primarily a body of people living the life that is in Christ. The ruined dormitory, the ruined refectory, the ruined kitchen, the ruined library were typical of the real problems that face the Church in the world to-day and which are to be found where men and women live and work and eat. To carry the roof of the Church over all the building of men's daily life, to open up a door between the place of worship and the place of work, to see the Christian life in a total unity—that was the task that the Iona Community undertook.

And it was a practicable task. George MacLeod's plan for the new community was that it should live together and work together on a common task only for the summer months and that its members should go back to their jobs on the mainland for the rest of the year. The practical task that The Iona Community undertook must therefore be one that could be carried on for a short period each summer and that could be completed in not too long a time. The work of completing the restoration of the ruins on Iona seemed to meet all these conditions.

So the second reason that brought The Iona Community to Iona was the job itself. It was essential that the work on which the members were engaged should be a significant job, a real job and a demanding job. The Iona Community has never regretted that this has been its practical task. Their life has had to be fitted in to the demands of that work of rebuilding. They have been held to practical issues by the demands of wood and stone. They have learned something of the disciplines of time and money. The Iona Community has learnt more than it can assess through this job of work which has been no toy and has allowed no playing with theories but has been simply a job to be done under difficult conditions and according to rigid standards of work. And into that job other things have had to fit.

It is work and not sentiment that allows the Community to bear the name IONA.

Then there was a third reason, and a lesser one only in that it was involved in the other two. Iona is a small and remote island. The Iona Community came to Iona not because it was an island but because Columba had come to Iona and because of all that had followed from his coming. But Columba had probably settled on Iona because it was an island. Certainly the settlements

c   33

of the Celtic Church were often on islands. It is doubt-
ful if Iona could have survived through the centuries if it
had been on the mainland of Argyll. It is certain that if
the Iona Community had settled for its summer work in
some valley of Argyll or Perthshire on the road to
Edinburgh and Glasgow its story would have been very
different and it would have missed a lot.

For living on Iona is rather like living on a ship.
You cannot escape, as you can in the city, from the
tensions of common life by going to the pictures or by
changing your company. There are no amusements
except those that you make with the people with whom
you live. And it is not always easy to leave the island
just when you want.

The purpose of The Iona Community was for men to
learn how to live and work together. The work of
restoration of the ruined buildings was a real job but
the object of The Iona Community was not simply to
get that work done. Its object was, through that real
work of building, to learn how the Church should live
and work in the world to-day.

It was not an easy thing to bring some young ministers
and some young craftsmen together and set them to live
and work on a small island. Neither group was trained
for this kind of life. And the training each group had
received did not make it easy for the one to co-operate
with the other. It was difficult on an island. It would
have been impossible anywhere else.

There was no place for the Community but Iona.

Chapter Four

THE MEMBERS OF THE IONA COMMUNITY

THE first members of The Iona Community were those few men who came with George MacLeod to Iona in the early summer of 1938. They were uncertain what the future would hold for them. They were not sure what would be the life of the community of which they had become members. But certain things were clear and these things have remained with but little change.

By joining The Iona Community they had committed themselves to each other in a quite definite way. More specifically they had committed themselves to share on Iona for that summer an intimate life of work and worship. In the discipline and demands of that life there was no difference between craftsmen and ministers. At the end of the summer, when they went back to the mainland, there would be a difference. The craftsmen would go back to their trade on the mainland trusting to find a job. The ministers would go for two years to jobs chosen for them as assistants in selected parishes in the industrial areas. But each month during winter they would all meet for discussion of their personal discipline and of the work in which they were engaged, and so they would maintain their commitment to each other.

The Iona Community has grown from that small beginning to a membership of well over a hundred. With that growth in membership its life has inevitably become much more complex. In its membership there is now an age range of almost a generation. Most of the members are now married and their family circumstances vary greatly. Its members are scattered all over Scotland and there are nearly a score of them overseas and a few in England and Ireland. Its minister members are working in all sorts of parishes, though most of them are in the industrial belt of central Scotland. But, for all that complexity and scattering, the simple pattern of that first year remains the basic pattern of The Iona Community's life.

The basic membership is still composed of craftsmen and ministers. The main aim of The Iona Community's work is still directed at the needs of our industrial society, though now we see these needs as not confined to those parishes most heavily industrialized. We now see that our whole life is fundamentally affected by the accelerating processes of industry. We would see the problem of rural Scotland as part of the problem of our industrial society. And with that realization the membership of The Iona Community has been considerably widened. It is not now exclusively confined to industrial workers and to ministers; there are now those in the membership of The Iona Community whose craft lies in other lines—in teaching, in politics, in publishing. But still the test of membership lies in terms of work and not merely of opinion. When a man applies for full membership of The Iona Community it is never enough that he should profess acceptance of the ideas held by the members of the Community—and, indeed, that has never been asked of any. Nor is it enough that he should confess a great desire to be a member. His membership must be seen to have validity in terms of his own work. The Iona Community is not an association of like-minded individuals. It is a community of men who see the Community to which they belong as having a particular task to do and who see themselves as each engaged on a particular task which has a bearing on the common task of the Community.

The primary and regular condition for membership of The Iona Community is still residence on Iona for a summer. In vastly different conditions each set of new members must repeat the experience of the first pioneers. That life of common work and worship on Iona is the one experience that all members share. The life that they now share in summer has become much fuller, much richer, much more disciplined. The labour is more regular and the study more ordered. The new minister members now share in the conduct of daily worship in the Abbey in a way unknown in the earlier years. And the season on Iona is longer: three months instead of the two of the wartime years. And for those craftsmen—masons and joiners—who work on the building, it is no longer a matter of coming up for the summer and then going back to the mainland; they are on Iona the whole year round. It is not merely that the demands of the work have made the original simple plan more complex and elaborate and so made it essential to have more men on Iona for a longer period. It is rather that we now know that it is in the demands of the work that we find a real, and not an artificial, life together, and know that one who has not shared that life can never really be a member of The Iona Community. In a very distinct way the life of The Iona Community has been built up in the building up of stone and wood. Each year's new men are identified with a particular stage of wall or roof. And the fact that each year has been engaged in a different task, and that each stage has depended on what has gone before and will be complete only by the work of those who come after, has helped us to know that in the common life of the Community there must be great differences, of work and of experience. So inevitably, with the advance of the building and with the growth of all that has come with that work in the life and the worship of the Community, Iona has become more and more the place to which its members come home and to which its new members come for training.

What we gain from this life shared on Iona is great.

What the craftsmen gain is perhaps difficult to express. What brings them and holds them is the chance of using their skill to the Glory of God—of knowing that what is expected of them is their best work and that the demands of another man's profit is not going to mean for them shoddy work; and also the satisfaction of working co-operatively and responsibly; and the challenge of being in such a strange society.

It is easier to see what the ministers who are on Iona for the summer gain. To them Iona has meant a radical change of life. More theological students have to-day experience of industrial life than a generation ago. But it is still a change after six years of intellectual study to spend every second day for eight hours working on the building of a wall or the digging of a drain. It is perhaps a strange thing to do as one's first activity after being licensed to preach the Gospel. It brings the realization that the presentation of the Gospel is not essentially a matter of intellectual study but of contact with men in the ordinary work of the world. And it is a valuable thing to have to learn to work with your hands—or, at least, to learn how difficult it is to work with your hands. It is also a valuable thing to learn to work alongside and under other men. No one would pretend that in their labour on Iona these ministers are experiencing anything of the tensions and difficulties of ordinary industrial life on the mainland. Indeed we should like to see theological students acquiring some experience of ordinary industrial life before they join The Iona Community. The craftsmen members of The Iona Community are not typical working men. The typical working man would never think of working on Iona, much less of joining a religious community.

But they are industrial workers. Their life has been spent in industry. They are representative of the men in the parishes to which the ministers will go—the many who do not go to church and the few who do. It is a valuable experience for ministers to work alongside and at the direction of such men and to know them as fellow members of the one Community. It is certainly most valuable for the ministers to realize how utterly uninterested these men are in their theological jargon.

It should not be thought that this co-operation of ministers and craftsmen is always easy. George MacLeod often says that the first fortnight after the first band of men arrived on Iona was the most painful time he ever spent in his life. And each summer we wait in expectation and in a sort of hope for a row to blow up. For it is when men cease to act a part and accept each other as they are that community life becomes real and corporate worship takes on a new meaning.

The pattern of life on Iona in the summer has thus remained essentially the same. It is still a life of work and worship shared by two roughly equal groups of ministers and craftsmen, though the life has developed into a more elaborate and, I think, more satisfying routine.

The mainland programme for new members also remains largely unchanged. The new minister members still go out as assistants for two years in selected parishes. But in the conditions of this further training there is one significant change. In the first year of The Iona Community they were sent out in pairs to work with the minister of the parish, thus making a team of three in the parish. It was felt then that the only way by which the Church could tackle the problems of the industrial areas was by a team ministry. It was felt also that only by the experience of a team ministry could the centuries-old individualistic conception of the ministry be broken down. These two convictions still stand unshaken. But 1938 proved the only year in which this plan of going out two by two proved possible. The next year war came and since then shortage of ministers has made it impossible for a parish to have more than one assistant. But that double stringency—of war and shortage—has forced the Church and The Iona Community to think more deeply about the problem. We have come to see that we cannot talk about a team ministry in terms of ministers alone. We cannot, indeed, talk about the ministry of the Church in terms of the ordained ministry alone. The work of the Church is not done by ministers alone. We have come to see the congregation as the agent of mission. We begin to see the meaning of the ministry of the whole Church. We recognize that the team is a wider thing than we at first thought.

The first and the main bond that binds the members of The Iona Community together is this experience of living and working together for a time on Iona. But that is not the only bond. There are two others: the regular meetings and the threefold discipline.

From the beginning The Iona Community has met in

monthly meeting on the mainland in winter. It has met to maintain the common life that its members have known on Iona. It has met also to discuss the particular problems of the life of members on the mainland and the progress of their work. At these mainland meetings there is always something in little of the life of the Community on Iona. There is always worship; usually a celebration of Holy Communion. There is always something in the nature of a common meal. And there is always work to be done. There is the work for which The Iona Community is directly responsible: the Youth Work of the Community, including the Youth Camps on Iona and Community House in Glasgow, and the Industrial Work of the Community, including Industrial Conferences and the Students' Work Community in Glasgow in summer. There is also consultation on the work in which the members are individually engaged. Most of them are engaged in the parish work of the Church of Scotland, mainly in industrial and down-town areas and in the new housing estates. There they are concerned with the building up of a new pattern of congregational life, with four main emphases——on Parish Mission, on Political Responsibility, on the Ministry of Healing, and on Worship. Just as on Iona stone and wood tie The Iona Community to the ordinary demands of corporate life, so on the mainland the work for which the Community as a whole is responsible and the work on which its members individually are engaged keeps The Iona Community from becoming solely engrossed in the discussion of principles or in the elaboration of theories.

The third bond that ties the members of The Iona Community together is its threefold discipline. The discipline is threefold in that it has to do with prayer and Bible reading, with the use of time and with the use of money. The present scheme of discipline has developed over the years. The idea of it has been there from the beginning and it has been the subject of constant discussion, experiment and argument. It is in essence the means by which the members of The Iona Community maintain, when separated, the life of discipline which they have known corporately on Iona. For that short time in summer is a time of discipline. It is a discipline in prayer and meditation. It is a discipline in the use of time and in the use of material things, of which money is but the symbol. But it is a corporate discipline. It is imposed and maintained by the accepted pattern of our life together. When in autumn the new members separate and each goes to his own parish, and all the members are scattered except for the small band of craftsmen who stay on Iona and maintain the morning prayers of the Community all through the winter, it is then that the problems of personal discipline arise. How is the individual to maintain that life of discipline by himself? This question brings the member of the Iona Community into the same position as the average member of the Church who is also faced with the problem of maintaining some kind of discipline alone.

The constant test in all the Community's discussions and experiments in the field of personal devotion is whether what is proposed is applicable to Church members in an ordinary congregation. The Iona Community in its experiments on Iona and on the mainland is not trying to find the pattern of life for an enclosed religious community. It is trying to find the pattern of life for Christians living in the world to-day. That is why its schemes must often seem to many so tentative, so slow and so compromised.

The first part of the rule concerns prayer and Bible reading. The Iona Community began in its first year with the assumption that all Christians, and certainly all ministers, did pray and read the Bible daily. Life together in one room revealed that this was not so. It was soon evident to the Community that very little help was being given to people in the Church in personal prayer and in the reading of the Bible and that what help was given was too individualistic. It was based on a moralistic interpretation of the Bible and on an extremely individualistic piety. It had little connexion with the ordinary lives of people to-day and indeed had as little connexion with the teaching of the Bible or the corporate nature of the Church's life. It was seen that our so-called "devotional" discipline must be tied up with the common things of life. It was particularly affected by what we were doing with our time and with our money. The true devotion of our lives was to be seen in what we were doing there. Our "devotional" discipline is the means by which we are held to that obedience.

So while The Iona Community went on to discuss the wider aspects of the devotional life it decided that it must have its clear "devotional" discipline of prayer and Bible reading. Its rule is that its members should devote half an hour each day to this. Help is given by the use of a lectionary, by the sending out of cards on which members report their progress—or lack of it—and by supplying a prayer-card on which are printed the names of the members and the topics to be prayed for each day. It is certain that it is this bond of mutual intercession that keeps the "devotional" discipline going. But while we struggle—and it is a struggle—to maintain this vestigial discipline, we try to foresee the new lines on which the life of prayer in the Church must develop.

The test of our Faith is in our use of time and money—and by money we mean all that money represents; all that we call our possessions. There is a sense in which time and money are our only possessions. They are the only things we have to give to other people. We cannot pray for anyone without giving some of our time. We cannot care for someone without giving some of our time and some of our things as well. That is why our constant excuses are "We haven't time" and "We haven't the money". We mean that they are in short supply because they are the only things we have got. Whenever we begin to be serious about our Christian obedience we realize this.

But The Iona Community was also forced to the adoption of its threefold rule by the immediate nature of its corporate life. Craftsmen and ministers had shared a common life on Iona and this had included a common time-table. On their return to the mainland the crafts-men would continue to work an eight-hour day. What about the ministers when they went to their parishes? They were free to use their time as they wished. The craftsmen were cynically convinced that the hours that ministers worked were very few. The ministers claimed that they never stopped working. Some kind of community was needed on the mainland between the craftsmen and the ministers; if not in their jobs then at least in the time that they devoted to them. So it was decided that each morning, as part of their devotional discipline, the ministers should plot an eight-hour day and at the end of the day should check how much they had in fact worked. Of course it is not as simple for the minister as it is for the craftsman. There is for him no clocking in and clocking out. It is left to him to decide what work he is going to do and to do it if he feels inclined. It is left to him to decide what counts as work and what does not. He is liable to interruptions that are often more important than the work that he has planned. In the morning he may have plotted a tidy pattern for the day's work but by the end of the day it is a mess.

The discipline of plotting the day's work and then of checking at the end of the day is extremely valuable, especially for men entering the ministry who have to change from the free life of a student to the demanding, but still uncontrolled, life of a minister. It is also a very healthy exercise for those who think they do a great deal of work. It is not so easy to fill the day with eight hours of solid work. Such a time-table means, for instance, no time for shopping or for personal affairs during the day. And, of course, one of the values of having this in our discipline is that we are forced to discuss not only if we are really doing a full day's work but also whether we are using our time in the right ways. It is worse than useless having a packed day if we are omitting our more important duties. What we need in the Church is a new sense of priorities in our use of time.

The Iona Community recognized from the beginning that in any kind of community there must be some expression of economic concern and economic interdependence. The Iona Community was also painfully aware that one of the reasons for the Church's failure to reach the men of Govan was the Church's refusal to be concerned with economic issues. If the Church was not concerned with the economic questions of the world to-day the Church would soon cease to speak to men at all. And if the Church was not at all interested in what her own members were doing in their economic lives— how they were making their money and how they were spending it—the Church would soon become a thing apart, a spiritual society, quite ineffective in the world and quite ineffective in the life of its members. For its own sake, as well as for its concern for the witness of the

Church, The Iona Community had to have some form of economic discipline.

But it is not so easy to find a scheme for a community the basis of whose membership is that its members have not withdrawn from their ordinary responsibilities in family, occupation and society. The discipline of a monastic community is something quite different. In it by their vow of poverty men give up their outside responsibilities and join a corporate life that takes responsibility for them. A scheme for a group of men who have not renounced their ordinary responsibilities, who are of different occupations and have varying family commitments, must be very different. Any scheme—such as the pooling of incomes—which seemed to lead to the Community taking total responsibility for the lives of its members seemed out of the picture. The scheme must be a pilot scheme pointing the way to what a congregation might do. It is not easy to find the way forward here. It is not at all easy to know how you balance economic interdependence with family responsibility. It is much easier to retire to a monastery or a *bruderhof* than to solve the economic problems of life in the world to-day. But this is the problem that the Church must face if she would be a missionary Church.

After various experiments The Iona Community has adopted a scheme which is obviously only a token scheme but which has at least led us from the endless discussion of theories into the practical business of dealing with money. By this scheme the members of The Iona

Community contribute 5 per cent of their disposable income to a Common Fund. Disposable income is income after the deduction of all allowances allowed by the Inland Revenue except the personal allowance, rent and rates (if paid) and Income Tax paid. It is possible for members in special circumstances to make a token contribution. The Common Fund is quite separate from the General Funds of The Iona Community and is used for such purposes as the members of The Iona Community may decide. It is a scheme of corporate Christian liberality by which we learn to make corporate decisions about the use of money and by which we are led into fuller discussions on the purpose of such liberality and into the use that we are making of the remaining 95 per cent of our disposable income, for it is there that our real economic discipline and witness lie.

When a man joins The Iona Community it is to these three things that he commits himself—the sharing of a common life of work and worship on Iona, participation in the meetings and the work of the Community, and the keeping of the threefold rule. He is not asked to subscribe to any theological opinions or political views.

The purpose of The Iona Community is perhaps best expressed in this prayer which was written for the Community in 1939 and has been regularly used in its worship ever since:

"*O God, our Father, who didst give unto Thy servant, Columba, the gifts of courage, faith and cheerfulness and didst send men forth from Iona to carry the Word of Thine Evangel*

D 49

to every creature; grant we beseech Thee a like Spirit to Thy Church in Scotland, even at this present time. Further in all things the purpose of the New Community that hidden things may be revealed to them and new ways found to touch the hearts of men. May they preserve with each other sincere charity and peace and, if it be Thy Holy Will, grant that a Place of Thine abiding be established once again to be a Sanctuary and a Light. Through Jesus Christ Our Lord."

Chapter Five

PROGRESS ON IONA

THE one thing on which everything else on Iona has turned has been the work of rebuilding. By it we have marked our progress. Into it other things have had to fit. Each stage of the work has led us into a new stage of our life in the Community.

To the members of The Iona Community the progress of the work has always been a bit of a miracle.

To set out to rebuild a ruined monastery by the labours of a diminutive community, without resources and without a guarantee, would seem foolhardy at the best of times. In 1938 it seemed to many to be quite mad. In 1939, when The Iona Community was but one year old, it looked as if its birth had been abortive and that The Iona Community would be one of the first casualties of the War.

During the summer of 1939, through all the forecasts and the preparations for war, the first bit of the rebuilding went on. After war had come, the little Library that stands above the vault of the Chapter House was finished and dedicated, that something complete should stand during the War and after as the memorial of a dream. Then, leaving the huts closed and boarded up and the

Abbey abandoned to its winter solitude, George Mac-
Leod and those who still remained of the Community
were ferried across the Sound to Mull on a dull morning
of a late September day. As they took a last look at the
Abbey it was enclosed in a rainbow. But the hope it
spoke of seemed a very distant hope. The flood of war
had engulfed everything and no one really expected that
the work would continue. The craftsmen had all gone
to the Forces. Many of the ministers were off on other
service. Who would be left to build an Abbey?

Yet next summer the Community was back and the
work went on. And so it was each year. Always there
were some to carry on the work. There were still a few
men coming out of the Theological Colleges. There
was always at least one craftsman available in summer.
One year indeed there was only one mason and one
minister with George MacLeod. Each year looked as if
it would be the last. And yet the next year the Community was back.

What kept it going?

Three things.

First, there was the encouragement that so many gave.
Indeed it was more than encouragement. There was
in it the determination that The Iona Community should
go on; and the promise of personal help. The Iona
Community had no funds. But hundreds enrolled as
Friends of The Iona Community to support the work of
rebuilding. And men offered to come up to Iona for a
week at a time or longer to assist with the building in the

absence of the members. Three groups were noticeable in those who volunteered to come. There were, first, many from the Services who came up on their leave. There were many young people who felt that this work of building was something that they could understand and in which they wanted to have a part. And there were many from other churches who came up to support the work. When we remember that Iona was in a prohibited area and that special permits were required to enter it, it is remarkable that the work went forward so steadily. For these three groups of helpers this work of construction, when so many were involved in destruction, was a sign of hope that they would not willingly see die.

Then, secondly, there was the encouragement of gifts. The work of rebuilding had been started in faith. Always the future had been uncertain, but never has the work been held up for lack of support. At each stage money has been given that has allowed the work to go on. In the early years of the War this encouragement was especially welcome.

And then there was the hope that was incarnate in George MacLeod himself. He had started The Iona Community in hope. We might say that he started it with hope alone. He had started it with the hope that men, craftsmen and ministers, would come forward each year to join in the work. He had started it with the hope that money would be forthcoming to sustain the work of rebuilding. He had started it with the hope that this strange little experiment would lead to greater things in the life of the Church. That hope was not based on any assurances or guarantee for the future. It was based rather on conviction and experience. It is the hope of which St. Paul speaks when he says that "experience worketh hope and hope maketh not ashamed because the love of God is shed abroad in our hearts by the Holy Spirit which is given unto us!" It has nothing to do with the hopefulness which is usually a waiting for other people to act and an expectation that something will turn up. So, for George MacLeod, hope is never free of apprehension. The Iona Community has had its constant share of doubts and worries. For him hope always demands energy and action. So ways have always been found and help has always come because his hope has been an active spirit.

The experience of these early years has confirmed The Iona Community in that hope. It has been training in a hard school. We have learnt that to hope is to plan and to act and never to dream unless dreams can be translated into action now. We know that this is true but we don't always live up to it.

The problem of continuing the work on Iona during those years of war was not caused only by the shortage of men. There was also the shortage of materials. So long as the work was only on the walls, there was no great problem. The pink granite of which the Abbey is built is local stone, from the Ross of Mull, and there was much of the old stone from the ruins available for use again. Freestone for the doors and windows had been brought to Iona before the War broke out. The problem arose when a roof had to be put on, for no timber was available. This need for timber became urgent towards the end of the War, when the section of the building known as the caretaker's house was finished as to its walls and needed a roof if it was to be preserved. There was no means of procuring timber. Then in the storms of September a ship bound from Canada for Liverpool ran into bad weather about a hundred miles west of Iona. She abandoned her supercargo of timber and reached Liverpool safely. The timber was washed up opposite Iona on the rocks of the Ross of Mull. Such members of The Iona Community as were still on the island went out with boats and rescued it. The Community was allowed to keep this rescued treasure. It proved to be just sufficient to make the necessary roof. In the absence of joiners the handwork instructor of Kilmarnock Academy asked if his building trade pre-apprenticeship class could take the designing of the roof as their theoretic work for the winter, and elect five boys to come up the next summer to put on the roof under his direction. So the first roof, of wood that came by miracle from the sea, was put up by schoolboys.

The next part of the building presented a graver problem. The stone-work of the Refectory was finished. It now needed a roof, but it was a very much bigger building than the caretaker's house. We could hardly hope for another gift from the sea. The supercargo of a fleet of ships would have been needed for so large a roof. The problem was solved by another miracle. A Norwegian naval chaplain, attached during the War to the Royal Navy, used to come to The Iona Community, in Glasgow or on Iona, on his leaves. He made it his task to interest the timber merchants of Norway in the work of rebuilding. Wisely he first enlisted the interest of Bishop Berggrav of Oslo. As a result, a shipload of timber sailed from Bergen as a gift from its timber merchants to the people of Scotland, in gratitude for the hospitality shown by them to Norwegians during the War. In ages past the Vikings twice burned down the monastery on Iona. It is a true joy that in these latter days help for the rebuilding has come from across the northern seas.

These miracle gifts from the sea and from Norway have led to other gifts of wood from elsewhere overseas. The timber for the East Range came as a gift from New Zealand. Wood from British Columbia is stored ready to form the roof of the Cloisters.

So each part of the building is associated with the interest and the generosity of Friends of The Iona Community in all parts of the world. Each part is also associated with the skill of particular craftsmen and with the labour and cheerful company of each year's group of new minister members.

As in the slow progress of the work each newly finished part has been brought into use, we have come to a better appreciation of the whole building and to a fuller understanding of our life together in it. In working on the restoration of the old buildings we have also come to appreciate better the life of the Benedictine monks who built and lived in it in the Middle Ages. We now know how much of their time must have been taken up in the mere business of living. The maintenance of life on Iona, the upkeep of the buildings, the care of guests must have brought to them far more acute problems than any we have ever known. We can appreciate better the nature of their life together and the place of their worship in it. And that understanding helps us to see the very different nature of our lives and the difference of the problems that face us in the world to-day.

Each new part, as it was brought into use, raised for us new questions about our life together and about the purpose of our Community in the modern world.

The first part of the building to be occupied was the caretaker's house with its roof of the wood from the sea. There was no question about its use. It was occupied by the then caretaker and his wife and three small children. This was presumably the first family ever to have lived in the monastic buildings. It was a clear sign that this restoration of the buildings was no restoration of monkish celibacy.

The second part of the building to be brought into use was the Refectory. As it was finished before the kitchen that was to serve it was built, the Refectory was not at once used for the daily meals of the Community. But it was the only place where The Iona Community had room to entertain those outside its immediate company. So, ever since its completion, the Refectory has been used in summer for lunch on Sundays when the Community entertains its guests from outside. And it has been used for the weekly concerts in which the members of the Community are joined by the members of the Youth Camps. Thus, from the beginning, singing and dancing have found a place in the restored building in a room where everyone can feel at home.

In 1956 the East Range was finished. It contains the bedrooms and kitchen and, on the ground floor, the Chapter House and offices. At last the Iona Community was able to find the centre of its life in the building it had restored. Its members had become used to living in a hut apart and found it strange to be under the same roof as the church. No longer did men have to go outside to go to the church to worship morning and evening. Only a door now divides the place of worship from the place of daily life. This makes the division between work and worship a much less definite thing. The noise of the one place is overheard in the other. And this is as it should be. But what is the real relation between work and worship in the world to-day? That is a question we must face.

The Chapter House is part of the East Range but it is distinct in that it opens directly into the Cloisters. It is the meeting-place of the Iona Community. Here the members and the visitors meet for Bible study, for lectures and discussion and for informal talk. It is here too that the stray visitor from outside is apt to land. So, as of old, it is the place of domestic discussion of those who live within. But it is also the place of meeting with those who are without. "All life is meeting": but what do we talk about when we meet? The finished and furnished Chapter House forces on The Iona Community these questions: What do we discuss with each other and with other men? Is any subject barred?

Still to be finished are the Cloisters. Already with the buildings around them complete we realize that they form the centre of the building. All doors and all stairways lead to the Cloisters. When they are complete they will be the centre of the life of the whole place. For us the Cloister has become synonymous with seclusion. We think of the Cloister as a place for quiet and meditation, whereas in a medieval monastery the Cloister was the place where ordinary work was done and where the world came in on its necessary occasions. What work is to be done in the Cloisters? How is the work of the world to come into the life of a community on Iona? This is another vital question.

So each part, as it has been finished and brought into use, has made us think how we should be building up a Christian social life in the world to-day. Let us remember that there are no easy answers. But let us also remember that we build up our social life, not in the air, but by the use we make of the buildings that we occupy.

This work of building is the chain that has held the years together. It has also given point and stability to our worship. For the worship has grown in meaning and fullness as the work has advanced. The continuity of the work and the continuity of those doing the work has given continuity to the worship. It has always been into the worship of a working and continuing community that the new-comer has come. The importance of that is quite inestimable.

Ever since the first members of The Iona Community landed on Iona in 1938 the members of The Iona Community have in summer gathered in the Abbey for worship at the beginning and at the end of the day. In the first year the forty-two stalls in the choir were about enough for the members and the few visitors who attended. Now at the morning service at 8 o'clock over a hundred will be gathered every morning, while at the evening service the Abbey will be filled almost to the back of the nave.

In those first years the worship of the Community was confined to week-days. But very soon the need was felt for a weekly celebration of Holy Communion. When men share all their ordinary meals at a common table the sharing of bread at the Lord's Table takes on a new significance and becomes an urgent need. So the celebration of Holy Communion on Sunday mornings at 10.30 has become the central service of the week for all who share the life of the Community. The service is according to the practice of the Church of Scotland. The experience of sharing a common life brings out clearly, and for the first time to many visitors, the social significance of the sacrament; from the invitation to the Lord's Table extended to any member of any branch of Christ's Church, "remembering that this is not the table of any one Church but the table of the Lord", through the bringing in of the bread and the wine down the new stairway from the ordinary kitchen, to the passing of the bread and the cup from hand to hand, each person being a priest to his neighbour. The Communion of Saints is a very real thing on Iona where every stone speaks of those who have loved the Lord in life and remained faithful unto death. The praise of the whole creation is a very real thing on Iona. But at the Table we know the centre of it all is our communion together with Christ.

The form and content of the daily services have become fuller and richer with the growth of the Community and the development of its work.

The first development was almost thrust upon the Community. Whenever the Community settled on Iona and began its work requests began to arrive for prayers for the sick. It was evident that the memory of Iona as a place of healing had not died: and indeed requests for prayer were coming to Iona before The Iona Community arrived. But once it was known that there was in summer a group of people meeting in the Abbey daily for prayer, requests came in great numbers. Requests for prayer can never be disregarded. In any case George MacLeod had long advocated the recovery of the Church's Ministry of Healing. Soon the Wednesday evening service was set aside as the service specially devoted to prayer for the sick by name. Requests for prayer came in from all over the country and from all over the world. The number was embarrassing. It revealed both the need of men and the Church's general failure to meet that need. One year we were forced to carry the prayers over into other evenings, so impossibly large was the number for one service. The demand is still great but, partly through the work of The Iona Community, many churches have begun to have some service of prayer for the sick. This is as it should be. The place where prayer should be made for the sick is in the place to which they belong and where there can be some response of care. But still requests come to Iona in great numbers, especially from abroad and from visitors to Iona who wish to join in prayer for their sick friends there. And this too is as it should be, for Iona is certainly a place of healing.

A later addition to the pattern of daily services was the Act of Belief on Thursday evening. It was felt that there was need for a place and time where those who wished might make an act of personal belief or dedication. This evoked so ready a response and met so obvious a need, especially among the young people who came up to the Youth Camps, that it has become a regular feature of the life on Iona and for many the climax of their visit. The emphasis which is made on Iona on what we do together in work and worship and on the necessity of social and political action does not diminish the demand made on the individual. Indeed it makes that demand in personal commitment greater, because it has to find expression in wider areas of activity and in new relationships with other people.

The first impact that The Iona Community makes on those who come as visitors to the island or as members of the Youth Camps is through the worship of the Abbey. And it is through the worship that the experience of life on Iona is interpreted. The appeal and the strength of that worship is that it is the worship of a continuing, working community. The core of the worship is the group of thirty or so men who are working on the building all summer and who come to the morning service in their overalls and working clothes and who go straight from the Abbey to their work. The opening responses of the morning service:

> "*Except the Lord build the House,*
> *They labour in vain that build it*",

are not in that setting merely conventional words. They have a literal relevance to the worship that follows and to the labour to which men go out. It is as those who labour in the building of the house that they turn at once to sing a morning hymn of praise and then in face of God's Glory confess their own inadequacy:

"*Jesus Christ, Son of the Living God, have mercy upon us—*
> *Jesus Christ, Son of the Living God, have mercy upon us.*
> *Thou that sittest at the right hand of God—*
> *Have mercy upon us.*

*Glory be to the Father and to the Son and to the Holy
Ghost—*

Jesus Christ, Son of the Living God, have mercy upon us.

"Then shall the Leader make confession saying—

*I confess to God Almighty, and in the sight of the whole
company of Heaven, that I have sinned exceedingly, in
thought, word and deed, through my fault, my own fault, my
own most grievous fault, wherefore I pray God Almighty to
have mercy upon me.*

"Then shall the congregation ask forgiveness for him—

*May the Almighty and merciful Lord grant unto you
pardon, absolution and remission of all your sins, time for
amendment of life and the comfort of His Holy Spirit."*

Then the congregation confess their sins and the member of the Community who is leading worship asks for
their forgiveness. After this mutual confession and
expression of forgiveness, there is a reading from the
Bible, another hymn of praise, and prayers of intercession. These end, not with the benediction as if the
service of God was now finished and men could go about
their own affairs, but with the Gloria; for the service of
God is continued in the ordinary work of the day, and
the benediction comes only at its close, at the end of the
evening service.

But if the permanent working community gives the
continuity that holds the worship to reality, it is the
variety of those who fill the Abbey week by week that

brings a great vitality and ties Iona to the ends of the earth.

They belong to three main groups.

There are, first, those who come as visitors to stay with The Iona Community for a week. They are the successors of those who during the years of the War came to assist the Community by their work. Many of them are linked closely to the Community as Associate members. At the beginning and the end of each summer season there are two weeks for Women Associates of The Iona Community. Apart from these two weeks the visitors at the Abbey in the summer are all men, for the amenities are limited. Some weeks are for particular groups. Each year there is a week for overseas students, and a week for men from industry. Apart from these the weeks are open to all men who wish to come: young or old, ministerial or lay, of any land. And there is a rich variety.

The second and much larger group is made up of those who come up to the Youth Camps. These camps are run by The Iona Community. One is in huts in the village. Another is towards the north end of the island and is under canvas. There is also a camp for boys at the fishing station at Camus on the Ross of Mull. These camps account for about a hundred young people a week during July and August. In July most of them come from the industrial areas, and a special effort is made to attract industrial youth and to use the camps to build up the youth work in the parishes of which Community members are ministers. In addition to young people from this country there are every year at the camps a good number of visitors from abroad. The camps have their own programme of Bible study, discussion and recreation. The worship of the Abbey is the place where all groups meet and find a common purpose. It is certainly the centre of the life of the camps.

The last group is the least easily defined: the visitors to the island. Many come to Iona because of the work of The Iona Community and because of the worship. Some come to the island for a holiday and then find the Community. For them Iona is the primary attraction, but many find that the life and especially the worship of the Community interpret the island in its beauty and in its history. And there are many who find in the whole experience of Iona some answer to their particular needs.

All these—guests of The Iona Community, Youth campers and visitors to the island—have their part to play in the life of the Community on Iona. The progress of the years is to be measured not only in the advance of the work or by the increase in the membership of the Community but also by the number and variety of those who enter into its life and support its worship.

With the buildings within sight of completion, questions inevitably arise about the future. What will happen to the buildings when they are finished? The Community's purpose was to learn through doing a job of work together: what will be the Community's task when the work on Iona is done?

These are questions that The Iona Community will have to face seriously in the next few years. In the past The Iona Community has gone on in faith, uncertain how the next stage was to be achieved but always sure that it would be in some unknown way. So now The Iona Community is not likely to come to a decision till the situation opens up. In any case there are still some years of work before the tasks already undertaken are finished.

But already three things are clear.

The first is that the Abbey belongs to the Church of Scotland. The Iona Community is responsible for raising the money and carrying out the work of restoration, but the completed Abbey belongs to the Church. This is as well for The Iona Community.

Then, the peculiar experience that has been given to The Iona Community has been gained through its members working together on the rebuilding and through the common life that that work has built up. If The Iona Community continues each year to admit new members and to offer them training it would have to find some equivalent to the work of rebuilding. This new work would need to be as serious, as significant and as demanding as the work of rebuilding the Abbey has been. What that work might be is still uncertain. Whether it could be on Iona or would be elsewhere is still uncertain. What is certain is that it would not necessarily be, and would not probably be, the restoration of a medieval building.

And, lastly, it is quite certain that Iona will continue to be a place of experiment, of training and of refreshment. With the completion of the buildings the opportunity for this will grow. The question will be how to have it centred on a natural, working life.

But these questions are for the future.

Chapter Six

THE WORK ON THE MAINLAND

IT is perhaps inevitable that in this story the emphasis
should be on Iona. Iona catches the imagination of
men by its history and by its beauty. Iona means so
much, and increasingly means so much, to the members
of The Iona Community that they find that they have
to come back to Iona to understand what their Community really is and to see more clearly what is the task of
the Church in the world to-day. When Iona means so
much to its members it is hardly strange that those who
are outside The Iona Community should find it easier to
see what The Iona Community is and what it is trying
to do when they are in Iona than when they are home on
the mainland. For on Iona The Iona Community takes
to itself a visible form in a building and in a life.

Without Iona there would be no Iona Community as
we know it; for Iona has moulded us. Without Iona
it would be difficult for people to see The Iona Community; for on Iona the Community finds a visible
expression. And yet on Iona you never see the members of The Iona Community at their ordinary work.
It is on the mainland that they do the work for which
they train on Iona.

At the beginning we saw how necessary it was to have some understanding of "Govan, 1938" if we would understand the origin of The Iona Community and would understand, too, its present form and activities. Yet we cannot go back to Govan in 1938 to see that picture. It is almost as difficult to see The Iona Community in its ordinary daily work as it is now to see Govan in 1938. This should not surprise us. Our ordinary daily life is the most difficult thing for us to describe. To give to someone right outside a picture of one's daily work is almost impossible. And yet that ordinary daily work is our true life; certainly the test of our life.

When the members of The Iona Community leave Iona with its clear picture of their life and merge back into the indistinct murk of life on the mainland, what are they doing? Or, to put it in another way, what are the men on Iona training to do?

If they were craftsmen going back to the mainland they would say that they were going back to employ their craft, to do the job for which they were trained as apprentices. If they were ministers they would say that they were simply doing the ordinary work of the Church, the work to which they were ordained or hoped to be ordained. They would say that they were trying to do it as well as they could and that their membership of The Iona Community and their life together on Iona had brought to them or strengthened in them certain insights which would now inform all their work.

In terms of the work of the Church these insights could be summarized under four heads.

The first would be a new sense of the corporate nature of the Church. The Iona Community came into being in protest against the individualism of our current Church life. What we have learned on Iona is that what we do together is far more important than what we do separately, and is the way by which we progress in our understanding of the Christian Faith and in the living of the Christian life. This sense of corporate life has to be at the very root of the life of the congregation in any parish. In their parishes the members of The Iona Community would be expressing, interpreting and emphasizing this in all the activities of the congregation. Without this there can be no sense of mission and therefore no true vitality in the congregation. The mission of the congregation to the parish, the congregation as the agent of mission, Parish Mission, Mission of Friendship—these have been the constant expressions of The Iona Community's first emphasis. They seem so ordinary that you wonder why they have to be made. We forget how insidiously individualistic has been our conception of Church membership. We go to church for what we individually get from the church: we go to church as a personal demonstration of where we stand as individuals; these are convictions deeply implanted in the minds of people in Scotland. If we are to get the idea across that the congregation is the only body of people who can carry the Gospel to their neighbours in the parish, and if that idea is to take so joyful a possession of their minds that they will undertake that task, a great change has to take place in the whole life of the congregation. The children's and youth work of the congregation has to change direction. It has to be brought into the whole life of the congregation. The Church has to be seen as the fellowship of all those baptized and not only of the adults. This conviction of the corporate nature of the Church has to find expression in all the activities of the congregation and in all the worship of the Church.

This means radical change in the pattern of congregational life. There can be no fixed pattern because parishes vary so much. But the parish itself as a form of ecclesiastical life is dead unless the sense of solidarity be found again and a new pattern for its expression. In the parishes of which Community men are ministers this attempt to find a more adequate form of social life takes many forms. But it is being made, in town and country parishes. In some parishes, especially in the new housing areas, these experiments in new patterns of congregational life come under the new and generic term of "The House Church".

What happens in the parishes in which such experiments are being made is that the parish is divided into small areas—streets or elders' districts. Every member of the congregation is a member of a group. The groups have regular meetings every three or four weeks. The meeting is led by a layman, though a minister may be present. The leader conducts Bible study and the worship with which the meeting closes. But the gathering is not primarily for Bible study. It is the Church in that street meeting for the purposes of the Church. It drinks tea, it discusses the needs of the people of the area, not only of the Church people but of everyone, and it undertakes to carry out the particular work of the Church in that area—and it reads the Bible and prays. In many parishes the roll is called at these district meetings, as a means of knowing what everyone is doing and to impress on the members of the Church that here in the life of their neighbourhood is the inescapable place of their Christian obedience. In such gatherings men will talk quite differently from the way they talk in church halls. They talk about the things that really concern them—their own activities and their own anxieties. As one group said when the suggestion was made that the meetings be discontinued for summer, "We can't stop for the summer. We're not an organization. We're just ourselves."

Three things are implied in the use of the term "The House Church". One is that the Church is in the home. We have too much come to think of the Church as the building. To the mass of people the Church is a building and what the Church does is what goes on in that building and only what goes on there. It is only by making the Church meet in the homes of the people that they will come really to understand that the Church is made up of people, not stones, and that what the Church does is what her members do in their ordinary lives in their homes. The second implication is that the large congregation of a town parish in Scotland is an amorphous body whose members cannot know each other and therefore cannot act together. Only by the creation of smaller units in the congregation can the Church become a body of loving people who know each other and know what needs to be done in their situation and how to do it. And thirdly an implication of "The House Church" is that the members of the Church are primarily concerned about their own Christian obedience in their own lives. The pattern of congregational life with which we are all familiar grew up last century and was based on the form of the philanthropic societies. The only justification of any Church organization was that it was doing good to young people or to people outside the Church. It is exceedingly difficult to get into the heads of Church people that their primary concern should be their own obedience. And yet thousands in the Church are looking for help precisely here. But they won't get any real help until the congregation transforms its way of life.

This insight into the essentially corporate nature of the Church's life is primary. But a recovery of the corporate life in the congregation will become but a new parochialism unless it leads out into a much wider concern for men. The love of the Church must be expressed in an active concern for the ordinary lives of people. The congregation must be interested in the ordinary activities of men and women in the parish—

in their work, in their amusements, in their social concerns. Its members must be equally interested and responsibly engaged in national questions, economic and political, and in the world's problems—of the world's hunger, of war and peace, of world government. In a word, the second emphasis that The Iona Community would make in the parish would be of the necessity of political responsibility. It would see this as an essential part of the Church's life and mission. But, despite the Church of Scotland's official advocacy, it is a line that is tragically far from the accepted pattern of congregational life to-day in Scotland. It is often a slow business to get these issues into the ordinary life of a congregation. It is a much slower business to get members of the congregation to see that a necessary part of their ordinary Christian duty is to join in party politics. This is the second emphasis that the members of The Iona Community would be making in their parishes.

The third would be a new insight into the pastoral work of the Church. The Iona Community came into being out of a concern for those who seemed quite outside contact with the Church. It was the realization that the unemployed felt themselves to be outside the concern of the Church that led to the necessity for new experiments. But perhaps more fundamental in George MacLeod's mind than this concern for the unemployed was his sympathy for juvenile delinquents and all whom society had injured and cast off. These were the people with whom the Church, if true to her Master, should be specially concerned. The respectability of the Church was one of the main barriers. The average Church member felt that he should have nothing to do with such people. So those who were outside the pale felt that the Church would have nothing to do with them and their case was so much the worse. For the one thing that they needed was to feel wanted. Only as they knew themselves to be wanted could they know themselves to be forgiven. The one thing that the Church should be able to give was this sense of community. Without it there was no real help for such people. But this help was what the Church was often lamentably failing to give.

The Iona Community shows its concern for such persons in the camps that it runs each year for Borstal boys at Camus on Mull and in the use that Alcoholics Anonymous are encouraged to make of Community House in Glasgow. But the effective action of the Church must be in the parish. It is integration into his own community that the Borstal boy needs. It is acceptance by his neighbours that the alcoholic wants. And this kind of pastoral care is something that Community ministers are trying to develop in their congregations.

These cases are but the signs of the ill-health of our society. Their care is part of the Church's Ministry of Health. The whole question of health—not only extreme cases of mental ill-health but the more ordinary cases of physical ill-health—has in the last few centuries come to be regarded as quite outside the province of the

Church and as having nothing to do with Faith. In the seventeenth century Jeremy Taylor complained that the people equated the parson's visit with the sexton's spade. To-day, as much through medicine as through theology, we have come to see that health is one, that it is of the mind and of the body and that the basis of our condition of health is in our relationship with those with whom we live. The sick have suffered as much as the delinquent from the feeling that they were outside the concern of the Church.

The recovery of the Ministry of Healing by the Church has been one of the marks of recent decades. It has been evident in all sections of the Church. It has invariably been manifest whenever the Church has been itself active in mission, for there can be no real mission without concern for the actual needs of men and men to-day are certainly afraid of disease. Mission must have to do with the whole man, with his body as with his soul. And health is not an individual thing: it is based on right relations. The Iona Community would see this pastoral work of the Ministry of Healing as an essential part of the life of the parish.

The fourth emphasis that is found in the parishes of Community men is on worship. The worship of the Church must express and be seen to express the fullness of the Faith and it must do so in living relation to the life of the people. And worship is something that we do together to confess and to grow into our unity in the body of Christ. The centre of that worship is in the

Sacraments. It is by their full and frequent use that a congregation is built up in active corporate service.

Nothing revealed in these four insights is unique. The Iona Community would never claim that it has been given any unique insights. It is only seeking to recover a total understanding of the Faith and a more serious intention of expressing that Faith in action. It has from the beginning striven to follow these insights in action and in so doing has come to understand them better. But it has done nothing that has not been part of the action of the Church in the past. It has perhaps pioneered in Scotland some lines of their recovery. But it has rejoiced to find others in Scotland and elsewhere who are following the same lines and in many cases have gone much further.

But it would claim—and this perhaps is its uniqueness —that these four lines must all be held together. It is dangerous for the congregation to adopt one line as its special concern and to leave the others alone. It is dangerous, for example, for a congregation to do everything possible in the way of healing and have no concern at all in political responsibility; or for a congregation to specialize in liturgy and have no interest in mission. To hold the four together in action is difficult, but it is the only way of recovery.

The Iona Community would not claim that these four insights or emphases together give an inclusive statement of the Church's life and work. Clearly they do not. But the Iona Community is convinced that if one of these is omitted then something quite essential is lacking in the Church's witness. These four emphases are practical warnings of things we neglect at our peril. And it is very necessary to have such signposts lest our witness become personally selected and increasingly narrower.

From what has been written it will be obvious that the main practical interest of The Iona Community is in the work of the parish. This is inevitable when we remember that most of the members of The Iona Community are parish ministers or assistants in parishes. They are in parishes because The Iona Community is convinced that the Church has to express herself in a life that is tied in the closest possible way to the life of all the people around her and in a way that confesses her responsibility for all these people. But The Iona Community is founded on the action of a parish minister who resigned the charge of his parish because he knew that the conventional activities of the congregation were not meeting the needs of the men in the parish. Unless ways are found to a fuller life in the congregation, the parish system is dead. Members of The Iona Community are at work in the parishes because they believe that new ways can be found.

But the parish system can no longer, because of social and economic changes, meet all the needs of men. This is no new situation. Men have for long left their parish to go to college, or to go to the Navy or the Army, or to go to prison. And the Church has recognized that special provision had to be made outside the parish system to care for such men. Chaplains were appointed to colleges, to the Navy and the Army and to prisons. The new thing in our century is that men and women go outside their parish to work. This has created quite a new situation because it affects not the few who can be given special treatment but the great mass of the people to benefit whom the parish system was created. So to-day the extra-parochial forms of Church work attain a new significance.

There are some dozen members of The Iona Community who are engaged in extra-parochial forms of Church work. There are several—both ministerial and lay—who are engaged in teaching. There is one on the staff of a theological college. There are several engaged in student work, and for years the care of overseas students in Scotland has been work for which men in the Community have had a special responsibility.

But industry is a vastly larger and more important institution than those institutions of education, the armed forces and the penal system which the Church has long recognized as outside the parish system. Modern industry is now so vast an institution and is so determinative of our whole life that something more is needed in the action of the Church than can be done by individuals. It is here that the direct experimental work of The Iona Community comes in. It is all fundamentally concerned with the problem of our industrial life. This is as true of the Youth Work of The Iona Community and of Community House in Glasgow, as it is of the Industrial Work of the Community. In face of the vastness of the task it is ridiculously small and tentative.

The problem is much greater than the effects of the geographical fact that most men now go outside their parish to work, that the men with whom they work do not share the same parish interests and that, therefore, the social and personal interests of their lives do not find their centre in the parish in which they live. This is in itself a big enough fact, which brings new problems to the Church. For the parish system is based on the assumption that the lives of people are centred on their homes, as indeed they were in the post-Reformation centuries in Scotland. But that day is gone and no system of Church life that is based on it alone will survive. This is not to say that the family can no longer be the foundation of the life of the congregation. It is to say that the family cannot be localized in the parish in the old way. When sport, education, amusement, political activities, shopping and industry have cut across and abolished parish boundaries it is quite artificial to think that the Church can preserve them. By attempting so to do the Church is in danger of declaring herself to be no longer the Church of the people but a group gathered from an artificially defined area.

The problem is much greater. It is not simply a matter of geography. The problem is that industry has developed in this country right outside the life and thinking of the Church and now the Church does not know what to say or do.   It is surprising that a Church which for decades has appointed chaplains to colleges, regiments and prisons, should only now, when it is too late, think of appointing chaplains to factories and industries.   Industrial questions scarcely appear in the Reports to the General Assembly of the Church of Scotland till after the First World War.   Industry in its modern form has grown up without the theologians giving any thought to it.   But it was not only the theologians who gave no thought to it.   The artists, the philosophers, the poets gave as little.   Industry was not a fit subject for art or poetry or thought or religion. It is scarcely surprising that men in industry should have felt left to themselves: left without guidance if they were in positions of influence and authority, left without care if they were down and out.   No wonder that the ordinary working man in Scotland was outside the Church. And the Church was not the only thing he felt outside.

The task of the Church to-day is not to act as if industry was just beginning.   If it were so the Church might appoint its parish ministers to act as chaplains in factories.   Its task to-day is to begin to understand what has happened and what is happening and to realize that what is happening is not just happening to other men but is happening to our whole life and affects us all.   And that is a job that cannot be done in the parish, though the parish must be concerned in it. Industry has to be studied in its own right, to be treated not as an unfortunate necessity in men's lives but as an essential part of the order of our society.

This means that those most responsible for the Church's thought and action must come to understand the situation in which men are set. It is thus necessary that ministers and those training for the ministry should come to understand this. This is as essential a part of their training as any of the more conventional sections of theology: it is different in that it cannot be solely learnt in class. Not that any true theology can ever be learned only from books or lectures. It may be that the necessity of getting out, if students are to understand the men to whom they will speak, will help them to see that theology belongs to life.

It was indeed the recognition of this that brought The Iona Community into being. The few years of its experience have only strengthened the conviction of the urgency of this need. In recent years The Iona Community, through the Students' Work Community which it runs in Community House in Glasgow in summer, gives theological students the opportunity of gaining some insight into the life of industry before they finish their theological training. Students, both men and women, and from a variety of Churches, live for twelve weeks in community in Glasgow while going out by day to work as labourers or factory workers in works selected for them.

It is for the same reason that The Iona Community encourages its ministers who are in suitable parishes to become industrial chaplains. It is not that the Iona Community believes that the Church's mission to industry will be carried out by the ministers of the Church. The Iona Community is convinced that the parish minister acting as an industrial chaplain can achieve nothing in industrial evangelism. It is rather that The Iona Community believes that, unless the ministers of the Church are in close touch with men in industry and understand something about the life of men in industry and about the social and economic facts of an industry, they will never be able to help the Church as a whole to understand and adjust herself to the situation in which the Church herself now lives.

But while the minister is important because without him no change is likely to be made at the present time in the pattern of the Church's life and thought, it is not through the minister that any kind of mission inside industry will ultimately be carried out. He is not inside industry. He may come to understand the life of men in industry a little better, but he is not able to do anything in industry. What is to be done can only be done by those who are inside industry. And the difficulty is that, because the Church has let industry develop as an untouchable area, those inside industry are apt to see their Christian witness as having to do only with questions of personal morality and with getting people to go to church. Men are aware that these do not touch the real problems of their life in industry.

So the main work of the Industrial Committee of The

Iona Community has been in the formation and encouragement of groups of industrial men in various localities. These have been gathered in most cases by the minister, but they are not congregational groups and they do not meet in the church. The first aim of the group is to get men talking about their own life and the real questions that arise in their life. Some of the men are members of the Church. Some are not. No attempt is made to put anything across. The whole aim is to make men feel that this is their group: that they can say what they want and must come to their own decisions. This is not what they expect from the Church. It is a common thing for such men to say that this is the first time that they have been allowed to say what they really think and to discuss their own problems in a group connected with the Church. These groups meet together in week-end conferences in Glasgow several times each winter, and there is always one week on Iona devoted to industrial problems.

The Youth Work of The Iona Community arose out of its industrial concern; out of its concern for young people in industry. The first direct piece of Youth Work undertaken by The Iona Community was the creation in the Canongate of Edinburgh of the Christian Workers' League. This, though still a small organization, is probably the most significant thing The Iona Community has done in Youth Work. It has had a formative influence on the general Youth Work of the Community and on its industrial work. It is a self-governing organization of industrial young people who meet in small groups and undertake a definite programme of Bible study and action based on the "See-Judge-Act" pattern. By this scheme they take up some fact or problem in their immediate experience, learn the facts about it, come to some judgment about them and decide on some line of action to be carried out by the group either corporately or individually. They also support their organization and other outside causes by a scheme of personal economic discipline under which all members pay 5 per cent of their wages into the funds of the League. It is the stringency of the conditions of membership that keeps the Christian Workers' League small. But it is that stringency that makes it effective. Its Bible study is serious. And it takes action.

The boy members of the Christian Workers' League in the Canongate showed in the early days a great interest in Iona and asked for a chance of coming up. An experimental camp was run for them in rather unattractive conditions. After their first camp there they decided that such camps should be continued and that the camps on Iona should be open to girls also. So again the contribution of the Christian Workers' League was decisive for The Iona Community. They laid down the lines on which the Youth Camps on Iona have developed until now six or seven hundred young people come up each summer to share in the life and worship of the Iona Community.

These are holiday camps, for they are primarily for

industrial youth who come to Iona in their short holiday. But they are concerned with what those who attend do on their return to the mainland. Those who wish become Youth Associates of The Iona Community. This involves them in a daily discipline of prayer and Bible study, in an undertaking to devote one evening a week to some political or social work outside the ordinary activities of their Church and in the opportunity of regular conference with their fellow-associates.

Both the Industrial Work and the Youth Work of The Iona Community find their mainland home in Community House in Glasgow. The House was opened in 1944 in the first instance as a centre of training for young people and has since then trained thousands of young people in the meaning of the Faith, in political responsibility, in the use of films and drama and in youth leadership generally. But its work is not confined to young people. It is a centre for meeting and discussion for Church people generally and for those outside the Church.

Chapter Seven

THE PURPOSE OF THE IONA COMMUNITY

IN this story of The Iona Community we have kept swinging between Iona and the mainland. This has been distracting. Many must have felt that the story would have been easier to follow if we had confined ourselves to Iona: that the story of Iona itself is interest enough.

But it would not have been the story of The Iona Community. That distracting swing between Iona and the mainland is an essential part of the story. For the members of the Iona Community that exhausting journey to Iona and back is an annual event not to be missed. If they cannot make it they know that it is their loss.

In that journey to Iona and back they confess that in The Iona Community they stand at the point of tension between the demands of the future and the demands of the present, between the vision of the things that are to be and the inescapable demands of the immediate present. It is a very uncomfortable position to occupy. It would be easier to read the signs of the times and build on Iona for the future undeterred by the pressing claims of mainland institutions; or to devote oneself with total absorption to these demands without a thought as to what is happening in the world and without a thought of the Judgment and the Glory.

The Iona Community would like to think of itself as an experimental group in the service of the Church. An experiment is pointless unless it is trying out new ways. An experiment is useless unless its results can be applied somehow to the present situation. There is no doubt that the Church has to find new ways of life and work if she is to fulfil her missionary duty in the world to-day. And if there is to be change, there must first be experiment; there must be those who pioneer the change. There is no doubt of the need of experimental groups. But this does not make their position any the less uncomfortable. Those who are fully engrossed in the demands of the immediate situation are irritated by those who point to the warnings on the horizon and talk of the need of radical change. Those who see the signs of the times find this involvement in the needs of the moment equally irritating. The Iona Community knows this controversy among its own members. It is well accustomed to the criticism of those outside who say: "Why get involved in all this outmoded parish work? Why talk in terms of the congregation? Why don't you cut loose and create the new community?" or of those who say: "Why all this diagnosing of our condition? Why not give all your energy to the work of the Church? There's plenty to do."

The Iona Community accepts this uncomfortable position. It would be worried if only one of these criticisms were made. It must not be failing too much if both are made.

The Iona Community accepts this position because it believes that it is at the point of meeting of future and present, of intention and act, that obedience is to be found. "Action now" has from the beginning been the motto of The Iona Community. This has not been to disparage thought. It is the expression of the belief that it is always in the situation in which we are set that we are called to act. It is always in our failure to act in the present moment that we fail at all. We fail, not because we have no idea what to do, but because we do not do the things that in our hearts we know we ought to do. We look before and after. We think of the times when obedience was clear and easy and hope for the time to come when things will be clear and easy again. But for the present we have an eternal excuse. And so we are lost.

And the present is always the moment of achievement. Obedience can only be now. It means nothing as a promise or as a memory. Obedience is often quite independent of seeing results. In persecution or in the darkness of despair men have known that the only thing that mattered was obedience. And obedience opens new ways because it leads us into understanding.

It is very easy to escape from this demand of obedience in the present. In fact it is almost impossible for us to face the demand. We fail not because the intellectual questions are too great and we do not understand but because our love is not strong enough. We are always trying to escape, as the members of The Iona Community know well, into the discussion of principles and techniques.

But the Christian Faith is not belief in principles. It is certainly not a matter of techniques. It is belief in a Person who acted in the here and now, in space and time, who was perfect in His obedience at that moment where intention and act meet.

It has been said of The Iona Community that it has emphasized the doctrine of the Incarnation. This has always mystified the members of The Iona Community, for they have always regarded this as the central doctrine of the Christian Faith. They certainly believe that we have to see this doctrine of the Incarnation not merely as an intellectual statement but as the faith that gives meaning to all matters of the here and now. For it is not belief in a doctrine. It is belief in Jesus Christ. It is the belief that He has acted and is acting in the world. It is the belief that He has redeemed the world; that He has redeemed space and time, and that following of Him is in the immediate present.

Now is the time. Now is the time of our failure or of our obedience. Now is the only time that we have to bother about. "Now is the time of salvation."

But it is the "Now" that terrifies us. As Christians

we do not know how to deal with the present. We have got out of the way of dealing with the present, even though it is only in the present that we can know Christ. We have been more concerned about our principles and our ideals. We have found that we can keep them clear only as we keep them distant. We are quite sure that we believe in peace for the world, plenty for all men and unity for the Church. But these ideals find no point of contact in our lives. Our difficulty is not that we do not want to overcome war and want and division, but that we don't in the least know how to begin to go about doing it. And so in our immediate lives there is a great vacuity. The ideals we profess and the actions we take find no point of contact in our industrial and political lives. We still manage to find a small area of action in our private lives. We make that the area of our Faith. And now we find even it invaded by vacuity.

Our salvation will not be found by the profession of larger and larger hopes for the future. It will be found only by incarnating our belief in some kind of action in our lives now.

The task of the Church, as The Iona Community sees it, is to face what are the real issues in the world and to find some way of obedience in action now. There is no use facing a problem if all that you are going to do is to be hypnotized by its greatness. The disciples of the Cross and of the Resurrection have no reason to be hypnotized, and no excuse.

The first thing that is demanded of the followers of Jesus Christ is that they find anew the way of discipleship for men in the world to-day. This is the first demand, because without it we can never begin and therefore never do anything else. Our idea of discipleship has become static and respectable and individualistic. We can only learn discipleship together, as the first disciples could learn it only together with Jesus. And that discipleship has to be in terms of the whole of our lives and not just in terms of Church affairs.

It may seem ridiculous to link such a seemingly ineffective thing as this with so terrifying a problem as the peace of the world. But it is the only thing we have to offer. It is the only way by which the peace of the world will be assured. It is "the faith that overcomes the world."

We have to face these two things together and as seriously—the peace of the world and our discipleship. We can do it only as we somehow break from the conventional pattern of our lives.

The second great issue that we must face is the problem of the world's need. All the questions of international relations come down in the end to bread. And the Gospel, too, in the end comes down to bread. The problem of the world's hunger is the most urgent problem that faces us. The Church cannot meet it by private charity. It is only by political action on the part of the nations of the world that the problem can be solved. The Christian's place is in political action. And this is where we in the Church have so generally failed. We can begin on the road to recovery only as we begin to be politically conscious in our congregations and in the Christian groups to which we belong. We in The Iona Community know how much more possible all this seems because we work and eat together on Iona.

And Church Unity: that may seem a declension after the vast issues of Peace and War and the World's hunger. But can we honestly say that we see any sign of its being first achieved? We take it last because it may well be for us the crux of all the others. It is certainly the issue from which we as Christians can never find any escape. We can blame no one but ourselves.

In Iona we know the imperative call to unity in the Church. In Iona much has been given to us. If we did not believe in the call to unity we would be blind and deaf.

The history of Iona reminds us daily of the witness of all the Churches. We cannot forget how varied has been the contribution of those who have served Christ on Iona. We can never believe that Iona belongs to any one Church but only to the One Church.

In the Abbey on Iona we have a building which is given for the use of all the Churches. The One Church is never going to become a reality to men, unless somehow they see it manifest in places and buildings. The One Church will not be a visible reality until there are buildings that are not The Church of Scotland or The Church of England or the Church of any other locality or denomination but simply and truly the Church of Jesus Christ.

And in The Iona Community we have the privilege of having within our membership those who are members of many Churches. This is nothing that we sought. It is an unexpected blessing with which God has blessed us. The Iona Community began as a fellowship of men within the Church of Scotland. Its work has always been with the Church of Scotland. It has since 1951 been officially integrated into the life of the Church of Scotland and is under the jurisdiction of the General Assembly of the Church of Scotland. Strangely, it was only when that happened that The Iona Community became ecumenical. In the scheme of integration it was stated that it would be possible for The Iona Community to admit to membership those of other Churches who wished to join provided that they did not number more than a third of the membership. We have never sought members from other Churches. We have no easy means to do so. But in recent years men from other Churches and from other countries have applied for admission to The Iona Community each year. To-day The Iona Community has within its membership two Anglicans (one a priest and the other a layman), several Congregationalists, and ministers of the Presbyterian Churches in Ireland, England, Wales, Australia, New Zealand, Canada, and the United States of America.

This ecumenical representation has been to the great enrichment of The Iona Community. It has been an extremely rewarding experience to have the young ministers of a variety of denominations and from a variety of countries living, working, studying and worshipping together for a summer and then going out into the same kind of work in the parishes in Scotland.

So through Iona itself, through the Abbey with its peculiar status and through the membership of the Community, we know that the unity of the Church is an issue that we cannot escape. We know this unity as a fact in ourselves. We see in the Church of South India a greater fact of which we have to take serious account.

The unity of the Church is not a matter of ecclesiastical organization. It must indeed have an organizational unity if it is to be a visible reality. But the unity of the Church will only attain reality through a new sense of discipleship. Then the unity of the Church can be seen, by the Grace of God, as the earnest and the instrument of the unity of the world.

Peace and War, the World's hunger and the Unity of the Church. These are great issues and The Iona Community is a very small thing. In the words of George MacLeod, The Iona Community would like to see itself as a "cradle"—a cradle in which new ways wherein the Life of God is manifest might be seen of men to grow.